Western
MONTANA

TEXT AND PHOTOS BY RICK AND SUSIE GRAETZ

A Montana Series

NUMBER TWO

PHOTOGRAPHY CONTRIBUTIONS BY:

Erwin and Peggy Bauer ▪ Randy Beacham ▪ Larry Dodge ▪ Guy du Von ▪ Douglass Dye
Chuck Haney ▪ Michael Javorka ▪ John Lambing ▪ Larry Mayer ▪ Neal and Mary Jane Mishler
Wayne Mumford ▪ Carol Polich ▪ Donnie Sexton/Travel Montana
Gordon and Cathie Sullivan ▪ George Wuerthner ▪ Salvatore Vasapolli

2

Arrowleaf balsamroot blooms along the Rocky Mountain Front near Augusta.

RICK AND SUSIE GRAETZ

Ross Creek Scenic Area, giant cedars in the Cabinet Mountains.

RICK AND SUSIE GRAETZ

Rick and Susie Graetz
P.O. Box 1707, Helena, Montana 59624
norockpub@aol.com

Design by GingerBee Graphics

All color, design and prepress
work done in Montana, U.S.A.
Printed in Korea
soft cover ISBN: 1-891152-04-1
hard cover ISBN: 1-891152-05-X

Front Cover:
The majestic Chinese Wall stretches for 13 miles across the central Bob Marshall Wilderness.
LARRY MAYER

WESTERN MONTANA

By Rick and Susie Graetz

Heading east across the simple grandeur of the vast Montana prairie a seemingly white wall shimmers in the distance...you can see it from almost one hundred miles away. The first travellers coming through these parts called this vision "the shining mountains." Those moving up the Yellowstone River Valley were seeing the Beartooth Range; the Rocky Mountain Front was the vista for the northern prairie voyagers.

The panorama on the plains stretches forever to the horizon, but now as the mountains are approached, it reaches up toward the sky. Montana east of the mountains terminates abruptly against the massive uplifts of the Northern Rocky Mountains and western Montana's eastern boundary begins. From these frontal rises its territory reaches west to the Idaho state line.

The widest stretch is on the south from Red Lodge, just below the Beartooth, through mountains and valleys 260 miles to Nez Perce Pass in the Bitterroot Range. In the central section, its eastern boundary is somewhat less delineated, here it is 220 miles from the hamlet of Two Dot to Lolo Pass. And from the peaks of Glacier in the north, it's about 120 miles along the Canadian line to the western edge. Dropping south from the Port of Piegan, east of Glacier National Park, an eagle will fly 330 miles before reaching Eighteen Mile Peak in the Beaverhead Range and Idaho's Lemhi River Valley.

Within western Montana's perimeters, the Continental Divide twists and turns through Glacier Park down to the Centennial Range and into Yellowstone National Park. From this hydrological separation, the big Missouri River is born. Waters flowing east out of springs and snow melt from countless streams feed the Jefferson, Gallatin and Madison rivers, at whose confluence the Missouri begins its journey to the Mississippi. Small rivulets of water and creeks draining from the west slope of the

Pink monkey flowers border one of the many creeks in western Montana.
GORDON AND CATHIE SULLIVAN

Divide power rivers such as the Flathead and the Bitterroot that fuel the Clark Fork, one of the major tributaries of Washington's Columbia River system which empties into the Pacific.

One writer described this western Montana country as the "Majestic Land"—and that it is! Mountain ranges of stunning beauty are interspersed with deep river canyons, broad fertile valleys, conifer forests and crystal clear lakes. The landscape mix is some of the finest on the North American Continent. The northern half of this terrain is defined with dense forests of pine, fir and tamarack and a multitude of lakes and streams. In the southern part, the timber stands tend to be more open and interspersed with large meadows of sagebrush and grasses. Blue ribbon fishing rivers meander through wider bottom lands.

Thirteen federally designated wilderness areas totaling almost 3,400,000 acres grace this province. One of them, the fabled Bob Marshall Wilderness complex, embraces the epitome of some of what the wild American West once looked like. The mountains of western Montana range from lower lying and timber covered to the alpine heights of the Beartooth where twenty-eight peaks soar above 12,000 feet. Numerous ridges and summits of other mountain chains reach beyond 10,000 feet above sea level. Glaciers fill high country cirques in many of the region's upper peaks; in the 1,000,000 acres of Glacier National Park, there are currently fifty active glaciers.

The western environs of Montana cradle an incalculable number of smaller lakes and streams offering some of the nations finest trout fisheries. Then there are the big waters—the Madison, the Big Hole, the Bitterroot, the Gallatin, the three forks of the Flathead, the upper Missouri, the upper Yellowstone, the Beaverhead and the Smith rivers—and Flathead Lake, the largest natural body of freshwater west of the nation's heartland.

Mallard duck.

NEAL AND MARY JANE MISHLER

Elk.

ERWIN AND PEGGY BAUER

Historians agree that the first Indians to settle in northwest Montana were the Kutenai (Kootenai) and shortly thereafter, the Flathead (Salish) and Pend d'Oreille. The Kutenai arrived in the early 1500s. The Salish and the Pend d'Oreille soon moved from the northwest to the Three Forks area and then further east toward the Beartooth. By 1800, the aggressive Blackfeet of the Plains had driven the Salish and Kutenai from the buffalo grounds east of the mountains back into northwest Montana. Hunting territories were jealously guarded by the various tribes. The Shoshone were in southwestern Montana before 1600. Eventually, with the advance of the white man into Indian lands, the tribes were forced onto a reservation. On July 16, 1885 via the Hellgate Treaty signed near Missoula, the Kootenai, Flathead and Pend d'Oreille were assigned to the Flathead Reservation. This land stretches from the lower half of Flathead Lake south to Evaro Hill just north of Missoula.

Lewis & Clark's Corps of Discovery opened the way for whites to penetrate western Montana as their journals and reports described the wonder and possibilities of the land. On July 16, 1805, the expedition followed the Missouri River into the mountains near Cascade. On July 19, 1805, Lewis entered a narrow and deep canyon of the Missouri. He wrote "every object here wears a dark and gloomy aspect. The tow(er)ing and projecting rocks in many places seemed ready to tumble on us... from the singular appearance of this place, I called it the gates of the rocky mountains." The area Lewis described is today's Gates of the Mountains just to the west of Holter Lake. On July 25, 1805, Clark reached the three forks of the Missouri River and named them the Jefferson, the Madison and the Gallatin after President Jefferson and two of his cabinet members.

Fur trappers were the first to follow the Expedition. In the fall of 1807, Finian McDonald entered northwest Montana and built the "Kootenai Post" near present day Libby. In November 1809, David Thomas established "Saleesh House" on the Clark Fork near Thompson Falls, and then the rush was on. Thompson explored much of northwest Montana mapping the Missoula area from the top of today's Mount Jumbo and probably was the first white man to see Flathead Lake (the Indians called it Salish). His maps of northwest Montana were remarkably accurate.

These traders were not settlers, they just passed through the country. Their kind though brought whiskey and disease to the Indians, decimating some of the tribes.

Bison graze north of the Spanish Peaks.
RICK AND SUSIE GRAETZ

Almost every community, large and small,

hosts a *fair and tests* of men and

women against *rodeo stock*

The fur trade continued to prosper until about 1840 when it began to slow. The colorful and somewhat destructive era of mountain men was dying. Catholic priests came on the heels of the trappers establishing missions at St. Ignatius in the Flathead in 1854 and at St. Mary's in the Bitterroot in 1884.

Gold was the basis of white settlement in western Montana. The first recorded discovery was in the spring of 1858 at Gold Creek just east of Drummond by brothers Granville and James Stewart, along with their partner Reece Anderson. In July of 1862, a gold rush to Montana started based on news of the state's initial big strike at Grasshopper Creek...Bannack the first Territorial Capital of Montana was created. As word of this and other finds reached the eastern United States and Europe, would-be-miners crowded onto the steamboats coming up the Missouri River to Fort Benton and then ventured overland to the gold camps.

One year after Bannack's beginnings, more than 2,000 people had moved into the creek bottom and surrounding hills. The population included some of the most famous characters of the Old West, as well as a collection of outlaws, crooks and thieves. Amongst these infamous individuals was Sheriff Henry Plummer and his gang of road agents. Their kind brought on the forming of the Vigilantes by the citizens of Bannack and nearby Virginia City to deal out frontier justice.

Other discoveries followed. In May of 1863, a find in Alder Gulch, 45 miles northeast of Bannack, proved to be the largest of all of Montana's gold strikes and spawned Nevada and Virginia cities. The treasure in Bannack played out and in 1865 Virginia City became the second Territorial Capital. In that period, 10,000 people massed into the rugged area.

In July of 1864, the "Four Georgians" out of Virginia City discovered colors in today's Last Chance Gulch...Helena came into being. By 1875 this "gold town" took on some permanence and replaced Virginia City as the Territorial Capital. In 1889, Montana was granted statehood and Helena became the permanent capital. And while gold was still king in the 1880s, Helena had more millionaires per capita than any place in the country...records show that there were fifty.

The gold period of the 1860s through the 1880s was a turbulent and wild time in Montana. But by the 1890s, gold began taking a secondary role to copper and Butte became a major town and producer of the metal. Considered one of the most prolific

Ride 'em cowboy.

RICK AND SUSIE GRAETZ

mining districts in the world, Butte earned the title "richest hill on earth." In the late 1880s it was also a prominant producer of silver, a byproduct of the copper.

As the precious metals played out so did most of the towns surrounding the mines. Only a few of the first camps, including Butte and Helena, prospered and lasted. But overall, Montana grew out of southwest Montana and its placer gold. As the miners established the first settlements, cattlemen soon followed. Communities came to northwest Montana a little later as a result of the railroad and the timber industry taking hold. While some gold and silver were found in northwest Montana, most mining was confined to the southwestern gulches and valleys.

Western Montana grew slowly from its beginnings, even through the early 1970s. However, parts of it have changed dramatically in the past 20 years. At one time, it was easy to describe the economy of the area as being driven by the timber industry, mining and agriculture. While the forest product sector is still the number one income producer, tourism and government employment have now moved ahead of mining and agriculture in much of the region. Transportation, education and health care are also having an impact.

Mining still plays a role in the Butte-Anaconda area and agriculture is important from Three Forks east through the Yellowstone Valley to Columbus. Ranching continues as the major way of life in the Big Hole, Madison, upper Yellowstone and Centennial valleys, the Big Timber, Livingston and Dillon areas, and the Smith River and Shields River valleys. Missoula, once portrayed as a timber industry community is also known now as a university town (the University of Montana) and trade center. Bozeman has added the college flavor to its attributes as Montana State University continues to expand. Tourism's growth is evident throughout the region, especially in Bozeman, Whitefish, Kalispell and Red Lodge.

Western Montana is attractive, not only for an incredible landscape, but for all the outdoor recreation it offers. Wilderness experiences that include a chance to see mounain goats, bighorn sheep or even possibly a grizzly bear or wolf, scenic drives, snow sports, fishing, hunting, floating and hiking are just a few of the myriad of activities residents and tourists alike enjoy.

Alpine flowers and Ramshorn Peak in the Tobacco Root Mountains.
GEORGE WUERTHNER

Abundant snowfall, plenty of vertical drop and no lift lines create some of the nation's best skiing. Big Mountain at Whitefish, Big Sky in the Gallatin Valley, Bridger Bowl near Bozeman and Red Lodge Mountain are all world-class ski areas.

Lower elevation weather is usually drier in the southern half of western Montana than in the northern tier. In the higher reaches though, each area receives plenty of snowfall ranging from 600 to 900 inches a year. Snow measurement courses in the mountains show anywhere from 100 to 150 inches on the ground by winter's end—up to 200 inches on the western border. The south is somewhat colder than the north and temperatures can drop to 40 and 50 degrees below zero. The national record for cold was set near Helena when the mercury plummeted to minus 70 degrees on January 20, 1954. Summer temperatures are warmer in the southern valleys than in the greener and wetter northwest.

Seasons here are well defined. Winter occupies the longest period—from five to seven months, depending upon elevation. The longevity is made up for by the beauty it creates.

Heavy snowfall and moisture filled clouds allow for portraits of snow laden trees such as the "snow ghosts" found in the Whitefish and Swan ranges of the north. Ice floats the rivers and the forests are silent under a deep blanket of white. Ski tracks take over from foot traffic.

Spring and early summer is the favorite time of most western Montanans. Melting snows and frequent rain showers bring a riot of color as wildflowers cover much of the landscape. The new green of larch and aspen stand out against the darker pine trees silhouetted against the still snow covered peaks. Fishing rods come out, kayaks, canoes, and rafts are launched, golf clubs are dusted off and Montana's sport—rodeo returns to the outdoors. Almost every community, large and small, hosts a fair and a test of men and women against rodeo stock. The long light and warm breezes of spring and summer evenings instill a sense of well-being in folks and the land.

Along about mid-September, with daylight fading earlier, a chill hits the air and the nights cool to below freezing. Snow dusts the upper peaks and yellows and oranges bedeck the slopes and bottom lands; first in the cottonwood and aspen trees and later, in the northern area, the tamaracks join in with their brilliant shades of gold. Low lying brush takes on a red and purple hue and the ducks and geese gather to begin their flight south.

Preston Park in the Siyeh Creek Valley, Glacier National Park backcountry.
JOHN LAMBING

The Northern Rockies of western Montana have turned to face fall and the approach, once again, of winter. The air is clear, the sky is blue and wildlife is on the move preparing for the long winter. Hunting takes over from the warm season activities and the Grizzlies and the Bobcats renew their annual pigskin rivalry on the football field.

The diverse weather, the magical scenery and a flavor of the West of yesterday combine to make western Montana a unique place in the Rocky Mountains. ■

Copper from Butte is a fitting finish for the state capitol's dome.
RICK AND SUSIE GRAETZ

French Creek and the Anaconda Range.
RICK AND SUSIE GRAETZ

Western Montana is attractive, not only for the incredible lanscape, but for all the outdoor recreation it offers

The Mission Valley and the Mission Mountains.

RICK AND SUSIE GRAETZ

Going for the big ones on the Madison River south of Ennis.

DONNIE SEXTON/ TRAVEL MONTANA

Storms can appear and disappear quickly in western Montana.
WAYNE MUMFORD

Sailing is popular on the larger lakes like Canyon Ferry, Flathead and Whitefish.
RICK AND SUSIE GRAETZ

A landmark barn near Pablo in the Mission Valley.
CHUCK HANEY

Grounded by a storm in the Flathead Valley.
WAYNE MUMFORD

24

In 1862, news of a large strike at Grasshopper Creek started a gold rush to Montana

From Territorial Capital to ghost town...as the gold went so did Bannack, today a Montana State Park.
RICK AND SUSIE GRAETZ

Hilgard Basin in the Madison Mountains.
RICK AND SUSIE GRAETZ

Georgetown Lake and the Pintlar Mountains between Anaconda and Philipsburg.
LARRY DODGE

Bald Eagle.
GORDON AND CATHIE SULLIVAN

Blackfoot Valley and Scapegoat Mountains.
RICK AND SUSIE GRAETZ

27

Ranching beneath the Rocky Mountain Front out of Dupuyer.
RICK AND SUSIE GRAETZ

There is still an authenticity of the "real" Montana to be found here

Wisdom is a watering hole and trade center for Big Hole Valley ranchers, fishermen and tourists alike!
RICK AND SUSIE GRAETZ

Bison rove the hills of the Two Medicine Ranch on the northern Rocky Mountain Front.
RICK AND SUSIE GRAETZ

Sunrise on Queen's Bay at Flathead Lake sets the mood for the day.
RICK AND SUSIE GRAETZ

34

The Yellowstone River east of Livingston.
RICK AND SUSIE GRAETZ

Two-week-old mule deer fawn in the Bitterroot Valley.
ERWIN AND PEGGY BAUER

A small side channel of the Big Hole River.
RICK AND SUSIE GRAETZ

Beauty in the rugged northwest corner of the state along the Yaak River.

RANDY BEACHAM

Beargrass in the Trilobite Range of the Bob Marshall Wilderness.
RICK AND SUSIE GRAETZ

Ruffed grouse in courting display.
ERWIN AND PEGGY BAUER

Crystal clear water in the Cabinet Mountains.
DOUGLASS DYE

40

Ringed by the Pioneer and Bitterroot mountains, the Big Hole Valley sits at an elevation above 6,000 feet.
RICK AND SUSIE GRAETZ

41

42

The Continental Divide twists and turns through Glacier National Park down into Yellowstone National Park

Upper Bitterroot River and the Como Peaks of the Bitterroot range.
LARRY DODGE

Iceberg Wall and Wilbur Mountain, Glacier National Park.
GORDON AND CATHIE SULLIVAN

Once known as "the richest hill on earth," Butte today has a personality all its own.
RICK AND SUSIE GRAETZ

Pine Marten.
ERWIN AND PEGGY BAUER

The Spanish Peaks as seen from the Big Sky Ski Resort.
RICK AND SUSIE GRAETZ

45

Colorful Lower Two Medicine Lake on the southeast edge of Glacier National Park.
RICK AND SUSIE GRAETZ

47

St. Mary Lake,
Glacier National
Park. DOUGLASS DYE

49

The weather has many moods,

often changing its mind suddenly

Beargrass seems to be one of the most favored of all western Montana's wildflowers.

CHUCK HANEY

East of Eureka.

RICK AND SUSIE GRAETZ

Red Rock Lakes National Wildlife Refuge serves as a haven for breeding trumpeter swans.
RICK AND SUSIE GRAETZ

Western Montana College in Dillon offers education in the midst of one of the finest outdoor recreation areas.
RICK AND SUSIE GRAETZ

The Gallatin River is a playground for rafters, kayakers and fishermen.
RICK AND SUSIE GRAETZ

The Gallatin Range
as seen from the
Paradise Valley.
CAROL POLICH

The seasons in western Montana

are well defined

Driving them home near Mcleod.
RICK AND SUSIE GRAETZ

Fall brings a nip to the air and color to the hillsides and valleys.
DOUGLASS DYE

57

Glacier Peak, Mount Villard and Sawtooth Spire reflect in Rough Lake, Absaroka-Beartooth Wilderness.
RICK AND SUSIE GRAETZ

59

Twin Lakes in the Crazy Mountains.
RICK AND SUSIE GRAETZ

Montana Hall on the Montanan State University campus in Bozeman.
RICK AND SUSIE GRAETZ

The Beartooth Wilderness is a haven for hikers and backpackers.
RICK AND SUSIE GRAETZ

The Garden Wall, Glacier National Park.
JOHN LAMBING

The protected habitat of the Centennial Valley hosts the densest breeding population of pereguin falcons and ferruginous hawks in Montana.
CHUCK HANEY

About mid-September, snow dusts the upper peaks and yellows and oranges bedeck the slopes and bottomlands

Rainbows over Yellowstone near Gardiner.
SALVATORE VASAPOLLI

Two universities, four colleges,

two vo-techs and one community college make

western Montana their home

Missoula and the University of Montana campus.
GUY DU VON

King of the wilderness...the Grizzly.
ERWIN AND PEGGY BAUER

Freezeout Lake along the Rocky Mountain Front is a popular refuge for migrating birds.
RICK AND SUSIE GRAETZ

Nevada City and Virginia City (just a mile up the road) give today's visitors a glimpse of life in a gold camp of the 1860s.
RICK AND SUSIE GRAETZ

A mountain goat grazes beneath Montana's highest summit, 12,799-foot Granite Peak.
RICK AND SUSIE GRAETZ

As the gold went so did most of the towns surrounding the mines

The Bridger Canyon and the Bridger Mountains accommodate hiking, camping, downhill and cross-country skiing.
RICK AND SUSIE GRAETZ

Room service, hummingbird style.
MICHAEL JAVORKA

Off the Beartooth Highway.
RICK AND SUSIE GRAETZ

A pastoral
valley beneath the
Pintlar Range.
WAYNE MUMFORD

75

Thirteen wilderness areas

totaling almost 3,400,000 acres

grace this province

The Swan Range near Condon.
RICK AND SUSIE GRAETZ

Bighorn sheep.
ERWIN AND PEGGY BAUER

The Mission Creek area and the Absaroka Range.
RICK AND SUSIE GRAETZ

Mountain ash sparks the shore of Flathead Lake.
SALVATORE VASAPOLLI

Built from the riches of the gold boom, the Cathedral of St. Helena graces the skyline of Montana's state capital.
RICK AND SUSIE GRAETZ

In the 1800s, Helena had more millionaires per capita than any place in the country

...described the western Montana

country as the "Magestic Land"

...and that it is!

The Lima Peaks near Lima reach more than 10,000 feet into the sky.
RICK AND SUSIE GRAETZ

The last light of the day tops the Salish (foreground) and Mission (top) mountains.
LARRY MAYER

84

Kintla Peak area,
Glacier National
Park. WAYNE MUMFORD

In 1805, William Clark named the three forks of the Missouri River—the Jefferson, the Madison and the Gallatin

The Jefferson River near Three Forks.
WAYNE MUMFORD

Snow ghosts atop the Big Mountain in the Whitefish Range.
RICK AND SUSIE GRAETZ

A Swan Mountain Range sunrise.

WAYNE MUMFORD

90

91

The longevity of winter

is made up for by the

beauty it creates

Hay Creek near Polebridge in the North Fork.

GORDON AND CATHIE SULLIVAN

Emigrant Peak holds court over the Paradise Valley near Chico Hot Springs.

GORDON AND CATHIE SULLIVAN

Ice floats the rivers and

the forests are silent under

a deep blanket of snow

The Bull River near Libby.

GORDON AND CATHIE SULLIVAN

Cougar.

ERWIN AND PEGGY BAUER

Mt. Jackson,
Glacier National
Park.
WAYNE MUMFORD

WESTERN MONTANA

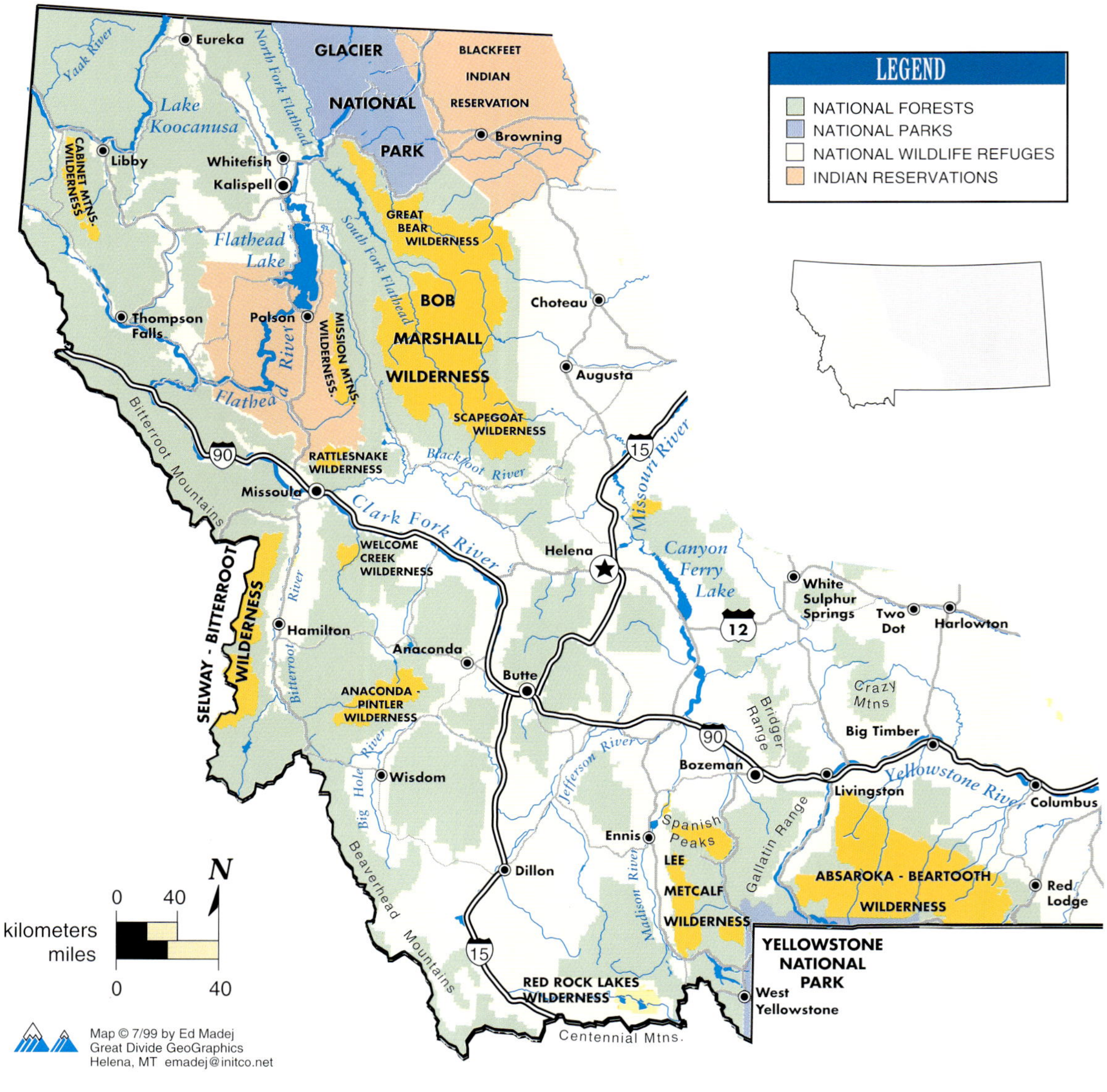